Awakening to Awareness

ALIGNING YOUR LIFE WITH
WHAT REALLY MATTERS

Eric Tonningsen

Published by
RockStar Publishing House
32129 Lindero Canyon Road, Suite 205
Westlake Village, CA 91361
www.rockstarpublishinghouse.com

Copyright © 2015 by Eric Tonningsen

All rights reserved. No part of this book may be reproduced or transmitted in any form or by in any means, electronic or mechanical, including photocopying, recording, or by any information storage and retrieval system, without the written permission of the Publisher, except where permitted by law.

Manufactured in the United States of America, or in the United Kingdom when distributed elsewhere.

Author Tonningsen, Eric
    Awakening to Awareness: Aligning Your Life With What Really Matters
    ISBN:
        Paperback: 9781938015311
        eBook: 9781938015328

Cover design by: Joe Potter/Cynthia Lay
Cover image and illustrations by: Tamara Vĭković
Interior design: Scribe Inc.
Photo credit: Courtesy of the author

www.EricTonningsen.com

CONTENTS

Introduction	v
PART ONE: *VALUES*	**7**
Being in Harmony	3
Outside Looking In	5
Connections: An Urging Force	7
A Letter to a Friend	9
Salving in Service	11
Inspiring Others	13
PART TWO: *INTEGRITY*	**15**
What Do You Stand For?	17
Excuses	19
Very Hard Things	21
Essence of Integrity	23
Walking Your Talk	25
Probing Probity	27
PART THREE: *SELF-BELIEF*	**29**
They Serve No Purpose	31
The Price of Perfection	33
The Opposite of Confidence	35

Reflections on Self-Belief	37
A Confident You	39
How You View You	41
PART FOUR: *TRANSFORMATION*	**43**
Transforming Yourself	45
How Easy Is Change?	47
Finding Your Life's Work	49
Appreciating Your Age	51
Being Open to Possibilities	53
On a Verge	55
PART FIVE: *AUTHENTICITY*	**57**
Yes, You, the Authentic One	59
Knowing Your True Self	61
Visiting Vulnerability	63
It's Okay to Be Alone	65
The Joy of Being You	67
Being Authentic	69
PART SIX: *SIGNIFICANCE*	**71**
Moments . . . Big and Small	73
Things along Your Path	75
In Those Five Minutes	77
Humility Helps	79
A Meaningful Life Trumps	81
What Really Matters	83
PART SEVEN: *HOW*	**85**
Getting from Here to There	87
Acknowledgments	89

INTRODUCTION

This book, as its title implies, is about creating awareness. It is about awakening ourselves to what really matters in our finite lifetimes. And it shares common sense considerations about what can happen when we effect purposeful change.

The impetus for *Awakening to Awareness* comes from decades of listening to friends, professional colleagues, and people in everyday encounters who have expressed dissatisfaction with their endless grinds to achieve and acquire. It was not and is not simply a matter of keeping up with the Joneses; it was and is the drive to possess even more money, prestige, and notoriety. This perpetual pursuit will not likely surprise us when we acknowledge how our society and Western culture encourage the accumulation of material success.

In my coaching practice, I often hear clients lament having important moments and truly significant experiences slip through their fingers . . . and lives. When I finally paused and gave intentional attention to these emotional sirens, my own awareness of what really matters began its slow yet steady emergence.

In 2013, I launched a blog titled *Eric Tonningsen's Awakening to Awareness* (http://tonningsen.wordpress.com). In addition to this book's first six chapters, the blog focuses on a dozen topics that I believe contribute to the fabric of what really matters.

A radio show with the same name soon followed, although with a slight twist: it targeted Baby Boomers and ways in which members of that generational cohort could potentially realign their lives. More than one year's worth of podcasts can still be accessed and listened to on iTunes (https://itunes.apple.com/cy/podcast/awakening-to-awareness/id733790197?mt=2).

This labor of love (aren't all literary efforts?) is an outgrowth of the blog. I reread more than 300 of my posts and selected 37 to share herein. I hold that these themes embody qualities of meaningful and significant consequence and are, to me, foci worthy of our limited time, selective attention spans, and personal choice.

With my business, blog, podcasts, speaking events, and now this book, I have two objectives: (1) to inspire you to reconsider what truly matters in our lives and (2) to invite you to realign with your heart, with compassionate actions, and with the plain beauty of being in service to others.

Simply put, I'm just here to stir your soul.

August 29, 2015

PART ONE

Values

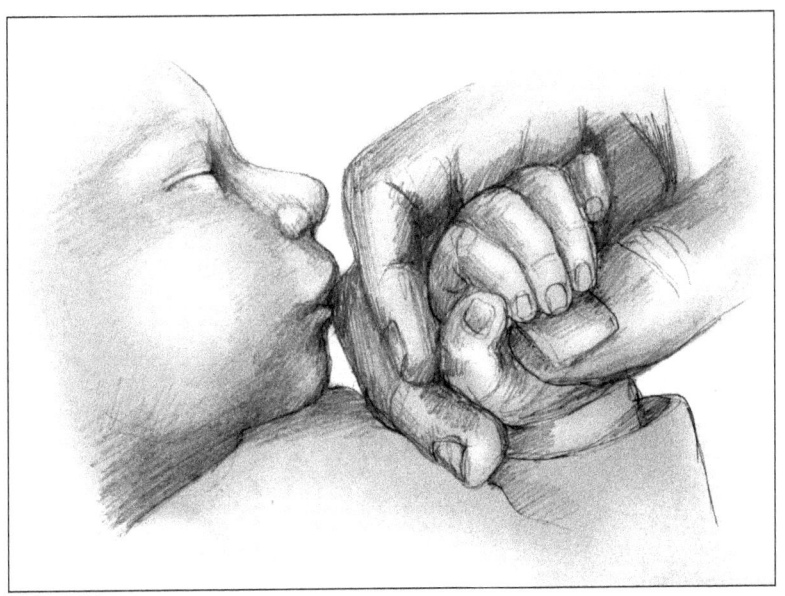

Being in Harmony

"When you find that your life is out of alignment with your grandest idea of yourself, seek to change it."

—Neale Donald Walsch

Life is ever-changing. Fair statement? Most of us are experiencing the shifting sands of life transitions. And there are times when we feel lost or when some things feel "off." Yet we are in control of our lives. We are in control of our actions. We are in control of our choices.

More fair statements (in my mind) include the following: Taking charge of yourself by being accountable and accepting responsibility for your actions are hallmarks of a strong character. Living your life in alignment with your values is not always an easy course to follow. Many difficult decisions must be made as we transit life. So we periodically ask ourselves, did I do, or am I doing, the right thing?

When faced with constant change, it might be time to embrace the idea that everything you once valued as important may not be what you value now.

When you are in the midst of a life transition, or even when you're not, it's essential to take stock of your values and then do whatever you can to align your life with your most core values. Living in harmony with those values paves the way for, if not ensures, happiness and peace of mind. Some people call this "living authentically."

In my mind, the heart is what represents your values, the things that are most important to you. When other parts of our being are not aligned with our values (e.g., when we make a different choice or take a different path), we experience disharmony, which can lead to feelings of frustration, confusion, or unhappiness.

It makes sense, then, that the more clarity you have about your values, the more rapidly you can identify why you are experiencing disharmony and realign yourself toward feelings of happiness. Ultimately, understanding your values helps you make choices to experience congruency, success, and happiness.

It is generally accepted that when you live according to your core values, you are in balance. When you stray from your core values, stress can build beneath the surface. Over time, you can come back into alignment with your core values, or you can rationalize them away. Or another value can overtake an existing one if followed repeatedly.

So here's a simple three-step exercise:

1. Identify a situation where your core values were tested or challenged.
2. How did you feel before you acted?
3. How did you feel after you acted?

Remember, you *are* in control... of your actions... of your choices... of your life. Create the change needed for you to *be* in harmony. You'll likely appreciate yourself even more.

Outside Looking In

"There are two sorts of curiosity—the momentary and the permanent. The momentary is concerned with the odd appearance on the surface of things. The permanent is attracted by the amazing and consecutive life that flows on beneath the surface of things."

—Robert Lynd

We all have invaluable human encounters during our lives, I believe. One of mine happened in June 2011 while traveling by train cross-country, and her name was Rose. She was considerably my senior and I, her captive audience for a while. I'll share more about Rose later. Suffice it to say, Rose stunningly grounded my belief in the adage "Don't judge a book by its cover," a quote attributed to the author George Elliot in 1860 that became popular in the 1920s.

Perhaps you have had the experience of encountering someone whose life seems so completely different from yours that you can almost imagine having nothing in common. However, if you go deeper into observing, you see that we all have similar things going on in our lives. It is as if our different lives are oddly interconnected. We all experience a range of emotions; many of us have money, relationship, and/or employment issues; and everyone struggles with different choices.

Your life and my life show up differently for us because we learn in different ways. One person may need to learn the value of money by having too little of it, while another may need to learn by having more than enough. We each learn about work and love through experiences that are customized to our perspectives. Though it may seem like some people have it easy while others are always struggling, the truth is that we are all learning, and it is difficult to tell, when looking only at the exterior of a person, what is going on inside.

From Rose, I learned how this is true with people from all walks of life. As we get to know those who seem different from us, we get to see how many of life's challenges and joys we have in common. We begin to look beyond the superficial—skin color, clothing preferences, social class differences, and the cars people drive—to the heart of the human experience. It is important to honor what is inside each of us and the fact that, regardless of how different we appear to be, what is on the inside is often the same.

For those interested in further exploring this, here are three suggested actions:

1. **Listen to the people around you.** People crave attention. People feel loved when given attention. Give love. Listening is an act of love.
2. **Talk to someone you think might be in distress.** You don't always need an invitation. You may make the difference of a lifetime.
3. **Live without limits.** Some limits are positive and necessary (think speed limits), but a lot of the limits we place on ourselves inhibit us from experiencing all that we have to offer. Limits like fear of reaching out to a homeless person or talking to strangers restrict the flow of kindness in our lives.

Connections: An Urging Force

"Omnia vivunt, omnia inter se conexa."
Everything is alive, everything is interconnected.

—Cicero

Ever grateful for my family, friends, colleagues, and clients, inspiration for this message comes easily. Whenever we pause for a moment and quietly listen, we find that life is calling out to us—inviting us to deepen our connection to ourselves and others, contribute what we can to the lessening of difficulties, and unfold into the people that we can be.

So what is connection? According to one definition, it is a sense of being part of something larger than oneself. It is a sense of belonging or a sense of accompaniment. It is that feeling in your bones that you are not alone. It is a sense that no matter how scary things may become, there is a hand for you in the dark. While ambition drives us to succeed, connections allow us to ally, to affiliate, to enter into mutual relationships, to take strength, and to grow through cooperative behavior.

We human beings have a fundamental need for contact with other humans. Our interactions and relationships with other people form a network that supports us, makes our lives meaningful, and ultimately enables us to survive.

Connections are important because they can help you when you are in need. You may never know when you may require assistance or advice. It is no surprise that mobile texting and social media sites such as Facebook are so popular. They are what they are today simply because the desire and need for human beings to meet and socialize with other humans is very strong.

Scientists who study brain function report that the human brain is wired to reward caring, cooperation, and service. According to this research, merely thinking about another person experiencing harm triggers the same reaction in the brain as that of a mother seeing distress in her baby's face.

Conversely, the act of helping another triggers the brain's pleasure center and benefits our health by boosting our immune system, reducing our heart rate, and preparing us to approach and soothe.

This is consistent with the pleasure most of us experience from being members of an effective team or extending an uncompensated helping hand to another human. It's entirely logical. If our brains were not wired for life in community—for connecting—our species would have expired long ago.

Another reason to connect is just plain common sense: In life, it's not just what you know but who you know. The more people you know, the more likely it is that you'll know the people you need to know, when you need to know them. Connections with others give us a place to contribute and to have our lives count for something.

There's a flip side, too. Life is lonely without other people in it. We are driven to connect with each other to ease our loneliness and increase our sense of place in this life. Isolation is where depression lives, and isolation is a killer. Just consider the fate of people in nursing homes who have lost their mobility, their vision, their hearing, and their interest in family. The more isolated they are, the less quality of life they experience.

Even with their importance, connections are not always easy to develop or maintain. As with other meaningful aspects of our lives, keeping connections vibrant takes ongoing effort. But isn't it good to know that connections are fundamental to many of our successes, our happiness, and the quality of our lives? We can connect in so many ways: through our words, through our smiles, through our hands, through companionship, through ideas, and even through comments shared on blogs.

So what are you going to do TODAY to connect or reconnect with others?

A Letter to a Friend

"A strong friendship doesn't need daily conversation, doesn't always need togetherness, as long as the relationship lives in the heart, true friends will never part."

—Unknown

Life whispers its meaning to us in the silence of the surrendered, open heart. It is there where I realize how much I value some friends. I find this silence compelling.

Sometimes it's hard to come straight out and tell our friends how much we love and appreciate them. We might feel awkward expressing deep feelings, even to our nearest and dearest, because it's not a common practice. We might get choked up and embarrassed in the process, or we might feel we will embarrass them.

Still, many of us have those moments when we realize how fortunate we are to have close friends, and we may long to express our gratitude. Moreover, it can be of tremendous benefit to our friends to be at the receiving end of our appreciation. At these times, writing (yes, writing!) a letter can help us say what we want to say without feeling self-conscious. Additionally, a letter gives our friends the space to really take in our expressions of love and the gift of being able to return to it time and time again.

As you sit down to write to a friend, take a moment to consider the qualities you most value in your friendship. It might be the fact that you always laugh when you talk or that you feel safe enough to confess your worst problems and always leave feeling better about everything. It might be the new ideas and experiences you've been exposed to throughout the course of your friendship. Whatever it is, take the time to express to your friend their unique impact on your life. You don't have to use big words or fancy metaphors; all you need to do is write from your heart, and that friend will feel the love in your heart.

Letters, which used to be somewhat common, are now rare. A handwritten letter makes a wonderful gift. You might simply send it or hand deliver it out of the blue. Whatever you choose, your letter will no doubt be received and treasured with gratitude.

So Gary and Jeff, while you don't read my blog, I miss you. Know that my letter to you will soon be on its way.

For those reading now, to whom are your letters going?

Salving in Service

"Life's most persistent and urgent question is, what are you doing for others?"
—Martin Luther King Jr.

When we feel bad, often our first instinct is to isolate ourselves and focus on what's upsetting us. Among our possible retreats are pity parties, contemplative pauses, or serious introspection. Sometimes we really do need some downtime, but many times, the best way to get out of the blues quickly is to turn our attention to other people. Yet while we are in service to others, paradoxically, we often find answers to our own questions and solutions to our own problems. We also tend to feel more connected to the people around us as well as empowered by the experience of helping others.

I have a friend, Dave, who, whenever there is a catastrophic event in the United States, will rush to that site to lend a helping hand. He spends little time thinking about the devastating losses, figuring he can always reflect on the situation after the fact. His drive is to be there, physically and emotionally, to be in service to others.

When he or we reach out to people who need help, we confirm that we are not alone in our own need for support and inspiration, and we also remind ourselves that we are powerful and capable in certain ways. Even as our own problems or moods get the better of us sometimes (and I know Dave's do), there is always someone else who can use our particular gifts and energy. They, in turn, remind us that we are not the only people in the world with difficulties or issues.

We all struggle with life challenges, and we all feel overwhelmed from time to time, yet we can almost always find salve in service.

In many situations, the people we are helping can knowingly shed light on our own dilemmas, sometimes with a direct piece of advice and other times without saying anything at all. Often the act of getting our minds out of the obsessive mode of trying to figure out what to do about our own lives does the trick.

Many great inventors and artists have found that the inspiration they need to get to the next level in their work comes not when they are working but when they are walking around the block or doing dishes. We do ourselves and everyone else a great service when we take a break from our woes and extend ourselves to others in need.

How are you next going demonstrate being in service? It doesn't have to be a magnanimous gesture. Little contributions are often huge to the recipient.

Inspiring Others

"Have you ever been stopped in your tracks? By a stranger who affected you profoundly?"

—Eric Tonningsen

Months ago, I briefly wrote about a woman named Rose. I committed to writing about her later. Now I am. Rose served as the inspiration for a story I shared over a three-month series of progressive speech contests. The following video link documents the last time I told the story in public, in May 2014: http://www.youtube.com/watch?v=QmRUQDaqCek.

If you watch the video, you'll better understand where this point is going. And yes, it has to do with how we inspire . . . and how others inspire us.

In May of 2013, I launched my blogging journey. Truthfully, I get more out of reading and viewing your posts than I do crafting and sharing mine. Virtually, I have met an amazing, creative cadre: people who take time to share what's on their minds and in their hearts, seen through their lenses and created on their unique easels. For enriching my life, a respectful tip of the hat to many in the WordPress community.

Here are three methods to consider for inspiring others if you are so inclined:

1. **Untether people.** Don't simply give people your advice. Give them the freedom to figure it out themselves. No one likes a micromanager or a know-it-all. If you're asked for help, share a rough outline to help the person move in the right direction, but leave something to the imagination so that he or she will have the freedom to fill in the blanks. Self-discovery will show people that they're fully capable and more powerful than they ever thought possible.

2. **Empathize with people's judgments, and reflect on their perspectives from an unbiased perch.** You can often find presence in the feelings and needs that lie behind their world view. Maybe they aren't changing, but you can create a space in which to transform your own judgments and expectations. You have the capacity to shift the opinions of others and reconsider relationships by simply focusing on yourself.
3. **Acknowledge the contributions of others.** You've contributed to your own life's successes, yet you're just one person. What about others who have added meaning and value to your life? It's not always your idea. ☺ Acknowledge other people's contributions publicly to show you are humble and appreciative enough to give them credit for how they have affected you.

PART TWO

Integrity

What Do You Stand For?

"Integrity is telling myself the truth. And honesty is telling the truth to other people."

—Spencer Johnson, MD

Not long ago, I was traveling by air. As I took a seat in the boarding area, I felt something protruding into my backside. Shifting forward, I realized there was a wallet wedged between the seat and my back. I pried it out and looked around to see if anyone had noticed and might, perhaps, acknowledge it as theirs. I opened the billfold to see if there was photo identification, and there was. I proceeded to the gate agent to report the find, and the agent called for the individual by name. He didn't come forward.

I soon boarded my flight, wallet in tow. When I arrived at my hotel, I phoned the owner. Getting no answer, I left a voice message explaining the situation and asked him to call me back. There was close to $700 in cash along with credit cards. Longer story shorter, the guy called the next morning, thrilled that I had found it. He asked if I would overnight express it to him, paying for the service using cash in the wallet. He also asked that I keep $100 as his thanks. I didn't.

Not once did I consider anything but returning the wallet to its rightful owner. Which brings me to the matter of integrity: having a conscience, being willing to do the right thing just because it's the right thing to do.

In this case, integrity went beyond speaking the truth and taking responsibility for how I thought and felt to the action I took. Integrity includes the authentic presentation of yourself to others (being sincere) as well as the internal sense that you are morally coherent. It also means acting congruently with your values—regardless of what those values are. Ergo, a person who has integrity does not necessarily mean a person who does "good."

The opposites of integrity are clearly negative: deceitfulness and insincerity.

Another way of thinking about being "whole" is that a person doesn't have integrity so much as they are integrity. In other words, it doesn't require some great feat to live in integrity. We just need to be ourselves, consistently. And in my view, there are many people in this world who are not genuinely well-intentioned at their core.

So how do you encourage and stay in integrity? Consider these exercises:

1. **Quit telling small, white lies to friends (including insincere compliments).** If you do tell one, admit it and apologize promptly. Monitor yourself and make a list of every time you tell a lie, even if it's a small one. Try to make your list shorter every day.
2. **Pursue humility.** Not the "Look how I put myself so low" kind of humility. Instead, make a full, honest effort to acknowledge that you don't know it all. With real humility, we can embrace our own brilliance and applaud that of others.
3. **Stop acting for the sake of others.** We've all done it. We don't go full-out or allow our true selves to shine because of what others might say. This has killed more dreams and paved the way to more destructive behaviors than many addictions. Your opinion of you is far more important than anyone else's. Strive to be the person you've always known you could be.

Socially, authentic people are well-liked. Are you? For what character traits?

Excuses

"Excuses are the tools with which persons with no purpose in view build for themselves great monuments of nothing."

—*Steven Grayhm*

Name one person, including yourself, who hasn't made an excuse. You're still thinking aren't you? Chances are we know few, if any, who haven't offered an excuse at some time. Excuses can be counterproductive and damaging and can leave people wondering about your dependability or integrity. Excuses may seem like rational reasons for us not to do something, but if we're not careful, we can allow them to keep us from reaching our goals. Too often we accept our excuses as reasons why we cannot accomplish what we set out to do, and instead of finding alternatives, we give up. You've been there, right? But if we can be honest with ourselves and take responsibility for our choices, we will begin to notice that we no longer proffer excuses.

When we keep our minds focused on our goals, we find that excuses fade away in the light of our priorities, and issues become challenges that can help us become wiser and stronger.

Sometimes we may give others excuses rather than be fully honest. We may think it is kind to tell someone we are willing to do something with them but then keep putting them off. This diverts our energy into keeping the truth at a distance while continuing a falsehood. But when we take responsibility for our feelings and express them honestly yet gently, the other person is free to find someone who is better suited to accompany them, while we are free to pursue the things we like. When we do this, our efforts can be invested in building better lives and relationships.

There's another way in which excuses rob us, and that is in the power of our thoughts and words. If we find ourselves in a situation, for example, where we are being asked for a financial contribution, but we use the excuse that we can't afford it, we can create and attract lack and limitation into our lives. The same goes for seemingly simple things like pretending not to feel well or making other false statements. We may think that excuses make things easier, but they complicate matters. When we can commit to our priorities, take responsibility for our choices, and communicate them honestly to others, there will be no need to make excuses and we'll be free to focus on things that really matter.

If you tend toward excuses, (1) face the fact that you are making or using them, (2) see them as antidotes for inaction, and (3) shift your priorities and act in integrity. Here are three common excuses and ways in which you can view them differently:

1. **I'm not inspired.** Inspiration comes from action, not the other way around. Popular leadership author and speaker John Maxwell says, "The whole idea of motivation is a trap. Forget motivation. Just do it. Exercise, lose weight, test your blood sugar, or whatever. Do it without motivation. And then, guess what? After you start doing the thing, that's when the motivation comes and makes it easy for you to keep on doing it."
2. **The production is taking too long.** Nobody ever said creative execution was sexy. In fact, it's grueling. The author Junot Diaz battled writer's block for five years before finishing his Pulitzer Prize–winning novel. The inventor James Dyson built more than 5,000 prototypes before he found the right design for his vacuum. And the list goes on. We must find joy in the process of execution, not just the end product.
3. **I've got to pay the bills.** Going with the status quo, we tend to give high priority to things like wealth and stability. And once we have them, it's extremely difficult to imagine life without them. But should these things come at the expense of pursuing big, bold ideas? Paying the bills won't necessarily earn you a legacy. ☺

Very Hard Things

"One of the hardest things in life is having words in your heart that you can't utter."

—James Earl Jones

I recently lunched with three friends. We enjoyed a casual conversation that, at one point, meandered into various thoughts and experiences about courage: the things no one else was doing, the things that scared us, the things that defined us, and the things that made a difference between living a life of mediocrity and one of outrageous outcomes.

It got a little deeper. We generally agreed that hard things are the easiest to avoid—to pretend they don't apply to us. We acknowledged a belief that ordinary people (like us) accomplish great things because they often do the hard things—the things that take courage. Being the demure one among us four, I decided to ask the others what the hardest thing was that they ever had to do—truly their most gut wrenching act or decision? And lunch took a very different turn.

I'm not going to go into what was disclosed. Each of us had a very personal story, just as you and others have. What I will share is that as I was driving back to my home office, I cried. Because I realized how fragile I have been and, at times, still am, especially when I must muster whatever courage I have and deal with life's hardest things.

Not always do people get the lessons and character they ought to out of the hard things in life. Some are not good learners in life's school. Some grow bitter in disappointment and lose some of their innocence. Others have their vulnerability pierced when they endure trial.

There aren't many ways to avoid very hard things. It's part of thriving. Yet there are counterbalances to dealing with life's biggest challenges; actions to redirect your energy and attention. If you seek or need to refocus, especially after having dealt with something very hard, here are three considerations:

1. **Find beauty in small moments.** Don't wait for the next big thing to happen—winning the lottery, having kids, getting promotions—find peace in the small things that happen every day. Enjoy the pleasure of sharing something you enjoy with someone else, holding hands with your partner, enjoying a quiet cup of coffee in the morning. Noticing small pleasures daily can change the quality of your life.
2. **Start a family.** I don't mean have kids. Make the decision to have a family, which means giving yourself fully to another person or several people. Risk being vulnerable by sharing your fears, quirks, and failures with someone else; you might find it makes you even stronger. Find someone or some people with whom you can share love, mutual respect, and trust.
3. **Practice self-compassion.** People often find it easy to offer support to others at the cost of being less compassionate to themselves. Research shows that people who are kinder to themselves, who don't get bogged down in personal imperfections and weaknesses, are more likely to be in better health.

Essence of Integrity

"Never separate the life you live from the words you speak."
—Paul Wellstone

Intending to write about integrity, I wanted to highlight someone as a pillar of trustworthiness—the epitome of integrity. Several people came to mind. Then, in a flash, an image of the antithesis was presented. And I found myself visualizing a diminished Lance Armstrong.

Personal integrity is not subtle; there are no shades of grey. You either demonstrate it, or you don't. Although he never failed a drug test during his cycling reign, Armstrong's legacy is now irreparably tarnished. He was stripped of his seven Tour de France victories and banned for life from competitive cycling. Lance didn't mislead the world; he lied.

Warren Buffet said it best: "In looking for people to hire, look for three qualities: integrity, intelligence, and energy. And if they don't have the first one, the other two will kill you." A person's dishonesty will eventually catch up to them. It may take years, but it is almost certain that at some point, there will be a reckoning.

Why, in so many cases, do individuals who have committed acts of dishonesty tell themselves they had a perfectly valid reason why the end result justified their lack of integrity?

Fortunately, there is a flip side. The movie *Jerry Maguire* exemplifies it well. In the movie, Jerry Maguire is a sports agent. He loses his high-end job as an agent to elite athletes due to a memo he wrote. Jerry felt it was wrong to talk his clients into doing something that was life threatening in order for him and his company to make money. He finally grew a conscience, and his newfound integrity would no longer allow it. The following is an excerpt from his memo:

> I wrote and wrote and wrote and wrote, and I'm not even a writer. I
> was remembering even the words of the original sports agent, my mentor,

the late great Dickie Fox who said: "The key to this business is personal relationships." Suddenly, it was all pretty clear. The answer was fewer clients. Less money. More attention. Caring for them, caring for ourselves and the games, too. Just starting our lives, really. Hey—I'll be the first to admit, what I was writing was somewhat touchy-feely. I didn't care. I have lost the ability to bullshit. It was the me I'd always wanted to be.

After his memo was sent to all employees of the firm he worked with, he was fired by a friend. Jerry turned that experience around and started his own agency with a focus on personal service for elite athletes, grounded in his values and personal integrity.

Invariably, we take on the traits of those with whom we surround ourselves. If we surround ourselves with people who are dishonest and willing to cut corners to get ahead, then we'll likely find ourselves following a pattern of first enduring their behavior, then accepting their behavior, and finally adopting their behavior.

If you want to build a reputation as a person of integrity, here are three actions you can take:

1. **Face the obstacles that cause you to lie or violate your moral code.** This might involve finding a more suitable job, facing your fears about how others might perceive you, or admitting when you've make a mistake. Recover and get back on track.
2. **Help others in need.** If you are in a position to contribute to the moral development of others or help them do something they cannot accomplish on their own, offer to assist. Help others accept responsibility for delivering on their promises.
3. **Identify aspects of your behavior that require change.**
Reflect on your interactions with others to determine specific areas in need of improvement. For example, if you are late for work every day and feel guilty about creating excuses for this behavior, this may be an opportunity to develop greater personal integrity.

Walking Your Talk

"Well done is better than well said."

—Benjamin Franklin

"There is no magic wand, my dear. In this world, if you want to accomplish more, you need to do more." That was wise counsel from a mentor some 20 years ago. Her advice was good across the board, whether starting a business, changing jobs, or simply checking a few things off your bucket list.

I was somewhat of a talker then. Reasonably accomplished, I talked a lot about what I wanted to *do*. Yet I found myself challenged when it came to fulfilling personal chores, completing deliverables, and planning for what I wanted to do. I was bluffing myself and others. And at some point, I acknowledged that I wasn't a *doer*.

These days, I'm on the other side of that fence. I collaborate with people who choose to plan for their personal development: people who have specific, realistic, small, and manageable goals. In hindsight, what I now see clearly is that an individual's growth is often attributable to designing a living (i.e., breathing or flexible) working plan versus simply thinking and talking about their goals.

Early on, I figured out that plans and outcomes are not built on good intentions alone. Positive perspectives help, yet intentions lapse when the distractions and demands of the real world are present. I remind people that the real work is in making things happen. And for plans and intentions to bear fruit, they require diligence, hard work, vision, application, self-belief, energy, and consistency. Plain and simple. Perseverance is essential, even if you lapse or come up short on your plan.

If achieving and contributing is an outcome to which you aspire, fairy dust and wishful thinking might make you feel good, but they're not going to deliver results. I used to be a great thinker . . . and a dreamer. I'm still both. What has changed, however, is that I now see these matters through a time, experience, and knowledge lens. And most of us have this vantage! We simply need to recognize what is practical, applicable, and right according to our own frame.

Walking your talk is undeniably doable. Doing so, you may want to consider these three foci, each of which can strengthen and empower *your* walk:

1. **Banish distractions.** Getting past distractions is one of the biggest obstacles to taking more action. It may not be challenging for people with enough willpower, but for many, stopping procrastination and focusing requires a lot more effort. Turn off things like your television and phone more regularly, and scale back your use of social media sites and Netflix. I know I am far more productive absent distractions. Perhaps you are too?
2. **Be a doer.** Practice doing things rather than thinking about them. The longer an idea rests without being acted upon, the weaker it becomes. After a few days, details get hazy. After a week, ideas get relegated to a back burner. As a doer, you get more done while stimulating new ideas in the process.
3. **Visualize success.** This is a tried and true technique. People know the benefits of visualizing their goals. Elite athletes do this all the time. In a similar way, create an image of the outcomes you want, and use that for inspiration.

Probing Probity

"Integrity is the essence of everything successful."
—Richard Buckminster Fuller

As a child, I rarely thought about integrity; I pretty much lived it. Like lots of kids, I was too busy exploring life to intentionally focus on ethical principles and behavior. The notion of being truthful was something my mother taught us. It seemed natural, "the right thing to do," even as I gradually noticed others around me taking less than honest actions.

But it was in the business world where I observed blatant dishonesty, largely in support of fulfilling shareholder expectations. Widespread questionable activity flew in the face of what I knew to be my values. On more than one occasion, my career growth was limited because I openly challenged unethical decisions.

Ultimately, I made peace with myself, left the very comfortable corporate cocoon, and chose to live life with integrity. This remains one of my proudest actions.

When was the last time you reflected on what was truly important to you? Are you living with integrity? Are you true to your core values? Do you even know your core values?

Each of us lives in a busy world. We strive to balance family matters, finances, our health, personal and professional relationships, and emotional challenges. Sound familiar?

So let's pause for a moment . . . Ask yourself what you most value in life? Here are two quick ways to discover this: Pay attention to the words you use to describe your life and the people you choose to share time with, and acknowledge your emotional actions and responses to those actions, as well as the attitudes and behaviors of others. Write down what you believe you value. Then look at what's presently in your life. Do you live according to those values, or are you living someone else's beliefs?

Stand your ground. Sometimes this is what it takes as you pursue your dreams. To stay in integrity while following your passions, you have to make choices along the way. Some of them were, and others might be, tough.

There may be instances when friends and colleagues, maybe even family, will have difficulty supporting your decisions. Yet these are exactly the moments in which you get to be clear about what living in integrity means for you.

There are plenty of ways to demonstrate being "in" integrity. Here are three simple ones:

1. Be willing to question what you do and how you do it.
2. Look for and find the best in others.
3. Understand that being "in" integrity isn't the same for everyone.

The Nigerian writer Chinua Achebe described how imposed Western "values" led to social and psychological disorientation of traditional African society. In his book *Things Fall Apart* (1959), he said, "One of the truest tests of integrity is its blunt refusal to be compromised."

You only have this one, physical life. And it's short! When you choose to honor your core values, you strengthen your mind, body, and spirit. If you have values that you have kept hidden to win the approval of others, then do you think it's time to reassess your life?

What are you choosing? Why?

PART THREE

Self-Belief

They Serve No Purpose

"There is only one cause of unhappiness: the false beliefs you have in your head, beliefs so widespread, so commonly held, that it never occurs to you to question them."

—Anthony de Mello

How many times have you felt that in order to do well in the world, you have to suffer and sacrifice? Certainly members of older generations have. This commonly held idea stems from a certain mentality inherited from ancestors who likely experienced this as true. Yet beliefs from our past-life experiences can also make an appearance in this lifetime. These are often the ways in which false beliefs take hold and don't let go, even though they are no longer relevant.

What we need to do is live our own lives in our own time and learn what is true for us, because very few truths prove valid for all people all the time. We are not our parents, our school teachers, or our bosses. Yet all too often, we choose to live the beliefs instilled by others.

It is not always easy to keep our minds clear of false notions, as it requires us to be clear about *our* beliefs. Still, there are times when these beliefs have settled deep in our unconscious minds, where they simply sit unquestioned. Think about it: How many times have you hesitated to do something because a "voice" from long ago said you couldn't or never would? Someone else's words can still have a disproportionate effect on your heart, your mind, and your reality.

Mistakenly, these beliefs act on us, creating situations and relationships that we regard as fate, when they are, in fact, simply our unconscious minds manifesting outcomes in the external world. As a result, we may wonder why we are not experiencing abundance, especially if we know we deserve it. Many of us have been there and fought that. Right?

To grow into our own selves, we need to examine the contents of our minds and hearts and get to the root of what we believe about reality.

When was the last time you considered such self-examination? In self-examining, we can benefit by rooting out any remaining beliefs that tell us we must suffer and sacrifice to do well.

There are many steps you can take to dispel false beliefs and reframe what is closer to true for you. Here are three:

1. **Shake out your belief system.** Challenge your long-standing, unquestioned beliefs. Ask yourself, where has this belief come from? What would happen if I let go of this old belief?
2. **Tell a new story.** What's your current story? How does it make you feel? If it doesn't feel good, stop telling it! Tell one that makes you feel inspired and positive. You *can* change the story.
3. **Step in a new direction.** Move toward and allow into your life new experiences, new energy, and new people. Let go of whatever isn't working for you.

Sometimes things as they seem aren't always true.

The Price of Perfection

"I am careful not to confuse excellence with perfection. Excellence I can reach for; perfection is God's business."

— Michael J. Fox

Just this evening, I had a brief exchange with a friend who is writing a book. It is a deeply personal story that she has been writing for quite some time. And she's done! But she struggles with something that many of us do—and not just with writing—and that is perfection. She keeps going back to the story, her words, and her emotions . . . finding yet more to change in her quest for perfection.

Perfection has different meanings for each of us. What complicates our relationship with perfection is our denial of two very basic truths: (1) We are not perfect, and (2) we are not, ultimately, in control.

In some cases, I still aspire to perfection. It is almost as though I am hardwired to do flawless work (though obviously not with my blog posts). ☺ When we make mistakes, we often believe that we are not meeting our own or others' expectations. And who wants to fall short? Yet if life is about experimenting, experiencing, and learning, then to be imperfect is essential.

I have a close friend who, when it came to my perfectionist leanings, once remarked, "Stop the insanity. Why are you doing this to yourself?" If you have ever been there or still have tendencies to perfect things and would like to change that, here are three considerations:

1. **Practice the opposite.** Be purposefully imperfect. See what happens. Arrive ten minutes late to work. Tell a lousy joke. Mismatch your socks. Laugh as you contemplate the possibility that imperfections are not only okay but life enhancing.
2. **Disclose everything.** There are few things more freeing than confession—not necessarily to a priest, but to a safe,

trustworthy friend. Write down everything you're afraid, ashamed, and embarrassed of, and read them to that person. You will likely be surprised when they look you in the eye and say, "I still love you." This is a first step to discovering how imperfect you are without your armor.

3. **Let go of your worries.** By obsessing about the past—what happened, what we think we did wrong (or someone else did wrong)—we are giving our power away. Be here now, and focus on creating an imperfect (yet beautiful) life for yourself. Focus on reasonable, achievable possibilities and practical, doable solutions.

The Opposite of Confidence

"Don't try too hard to fit in; you were born to stand out."
—*Anonymous*

Doubt—the bane of self-belief. Have you ever wondered why you're less than 100 percent sure of yourself?

Many of us can recall times when we've felt insecure about ourselves. Maybe it was questioning an ability to do something. Perhaps it was feeling self-conscious about the way you look. It doesn't really matter how these feelings manifest. What's important is that we're aware of our thoughts and how they impact our view of ourselves. Once we remember that insecurities are a normal part of life for most people, we may find it easier to step back from uncertainty and take a more realistic look at ourselves.

Have you ever been guilty of trying to "keep up with the Joneses"? The desire to better ourselves is a natural response that arises when we begin to compare our lives to those of other people. You've been there, right? It might seem, for example, that we do not have nearly as much going for us as our neighbor, best friend, or coworker. In truth, what we think we see in another person is usually what they want us to notice. They may be putting on a mask, trying to make things in their lives seem better than they are. If we were to look at their lives a little more closely, we'd likely realize that they are human, covered with warts that make them uniquely who they are.

Unfortunately, it's often our imperfections that we look at as unattractive, when instead we could embrace our flaws as what distinguishes us. Consider for a moment what the world would be like if our character traits were cloned, and no one had insecurities. Would it be a more interesting place? What if, when we felt our uncertainties begin to surface, we took a deep breath, paused to acknowledge our gifts or talents, and in doing so, became more grounded and grateful? Rather than react and retreat, we could intentionally allow our inner beauty to shine forth.

You *are* special. You have much to offer. Why compromise your confidence by doubting yourself? How does sacrificing self-belief yield anything beneficial?

When you hold up a mirror to your life and weigh yourself against others, you cloud your ability to see things that make you one-of-a-kind. Giving yourself permission to appreciate and believe in what you've been blessed with *will* make you feel more secure about yourself. In turn, you'll be able to use your gifts to the fullest. Wouldn't that be an interesting prospect?!

Reflections on Self-Belief

"I am not a has-been. I am a will be."

—Lauren Bacall

In the Fall of 2013, I competed in the Toastmasters District 23 (which includes all of New Mexico, West Texas, and the Oklahoma Panhandle) Speech Contests. My first-place award was presented by the President of Toastmasters International, George Yen of Taiwan, who presided.

I've had a couple of days to reflect on what propelled me to that stage and what sustained my drive throughout the two-month, progressive contest season. While I'd like to credit skill and practice (and they were contributing factors), it was self-belief that anchored and reassured me.

So how does my confidence differ from yours? Perhaps not at all. But I thought I'd share some self-belief qualities that you might want acknowledge in yourself, even if you don't see or value them yet. It is said that a self-confident individuals can openly talk about their fears, yet they don't let negative attributes hinder them from becoming the best they can be. Instead, they strive to improve their weaknesses and continue to hone their strengths. Individuals who believe in themselves stand out because they are not afraid to showcase their talents and skills. And I did.

Self-awareness helps, too. It is essential that you know yourself inside out. Self-awareness encourages you to take the initiative to change and challenge yourself, because it helps you realize you need it. Consider changing your mind-set. If your mind-set is full of restrictions and negative beliefs, it isn't going to help you improve your self-belief.

For your consideration, here are four ideas:

1. **Become an even better communicator.** People with strong self-belief know how to ask for what they want and to hear advice and counsel. It is less important for them to be right than to be effective. They listen more than they speak.

2. **Challenge your beliefs.** Examine your beliefs closely and determine if they are in line with the life you desire. If you choose, you can abandon negative beliefs about yourself and, as you do, realize growth in your confidence.
3. **Be open and attractive to others.** Confident people are usually drawn to one another. They vibrate their confidence in ways that attract good things and good people to them.
4. **Be your own hero.** Write down the attributes you admire in others (compassion, honesty, integrity, etc.). Make it a long list. The more you note, the more you'll begin to see the self-belief qualities you want to have. Begin emulating them, and be prepared to enjoy the feel-good benefits of being your own hero!

A Confident You

"Nobody can make you feel inferior without your consent."
—Eleanor Roosevelt

Each of us has one life. Would you rather spend your entire life doing something you do not love, just because of circumstances? Or are you focused on heeding that calling you can't stop thinking about and doing "it" to the best of your ability?

If you don't believe in you, who else is going to? This doesn't mean you have to be crystal clear about who you are and how you're using your personal gifts. That will come with time and effort. But it does suggest that if you're lacking confidence or have little self-belief, you will be less likely to trust and listen to the individual you've created.

Self-confidence, or self-belief, is generally considered to be the way that you feel about your abilities, skills, behaviors, and looks. Someone who has a high level of confidence may trust and be happy that he or she can complete tasks to a high standard, learn quickly, or appear attractive to others. Simply stated, self-confidence is having faith in yourself.

Yet many people portray an image of complete confidence to others while shaking with fear on the inside. This is a protection method often used to cover up a lack of confidence, self-belief, or other feelings about themselves that they'd rather not acknowledge.

A fan of simple versus complex, I also prefer to focus on "possessing" and "abundance" rather than "lacking" and "deficiency." If you are filled with confidence and self-belief, you are more likely to feel

- excited about new opportunities,
- respected by others,
- comfortable facing new challenges, and
- sure of yourself and what you want.

Professional coaches can often help people learn different techniques to explore their confidence and self-belief. Coaching supports an individual's self-image and encourages people to create more positive personal outlooks.

If you truly believe in yourself, so will others.

To get a sense of this, try being your own coach. If you notice doubts rearing their ugly heads, imagine that you (the clearheaded part of you) are the coach and that the anxious part of you is the person with whom you are talking.

Think about what you'd say to someone you really believe in if *they* started showing doubts. Sit down and say those same words to yourself. If you're about to go into a job interview and you "hear yourself" starting to express doubts, take a few moments to sit down, close your eyes, and motivate yourself: "Look, you *can* do this! It's natural to feel a little anxious, but that just confirms you care about what you're doing! You've got all the relevant experience and qualifications! Now get in there, and stop whining! Even if you don't get the offer, you're going to make me proud by giving it your best shot!"

Picture the decent, friendly, straight-talking coach in your mind. They're your unconditional ally! Is it someone you know or would like to know? Talking to yourself in these times as if you were another person (in the privacy of your mind) can boost your confidence quickly.

How strongly do you believe in *you*?

How You View You

"Your whole life is a message. Every act is an act of self-definition. Everything you think, say and do sends a message about you."

—Neale Donald Walsch

Most of us, I believe, have at least one or two facets of ourselves that we spend considerable time nurturing. They're often challenging efforts, in conjunction with personal growth and development. The other day, someone asked me what one thing matters most to me? And I couldn't immediately answer the question. My first reaction was to cite one of my key values, but something deep inside said, "You're warm, but it's not that." I sought time and promised I'd soon get back to her with an answer.

I'm glad I didn't rush simply for the sake of quickly giving an answer. When I later created space to reflect on the question, my mind was all over the map. I began to write.

- being happy
- certainty in life purpose
- knowledge
- fulfilling relationships
- smiling
- compassion for others
- love
- accepting defeat
- family
- continuing to breathe
- learning
- being passionate
- mindfulness
- time
- being empathetic

- health
- life itself
- curiosity
- and much more

It was while contemplating the "much more" that I discovered what matters most to me: *a positive self-view*. For me, having a positive self-view (others might see this as self-regard or self-concept) means accepting myself for who I am and what I believe in. It means having the courage necessary to make my own decisions and to live life in the way that's right for me. Absent a positive self-view, we tend to compare ourselves to others, feel insecure about ourselves, and become too sensitive to the opinions of others (though I admit to being a highly sensitive person). We also make choices based on other people's expectations rather than what truly feels right for us.

I've lived much of my life with a diminished self-view. Sure, I've been cocky and confident, but there were plenty of times when I was concerned about other people's judgment. Like many people, I've come a long way, yet among other perceptions, I'm still working on learning to love myself unconditionally. And for me, this continues to be challenging work.

If a strong(er) positive self-view matters to you, here are three considerations:

1. **Accept imperfections.** Perfection is a lofty intention, yet you need not start or end there. You've heard it before, but doing your best is an admirable goal. Focus on what you have achieved and accomplished and how you can draw on same going forward. Bypass what wasn't done or ought to have been done differently, and laugh at yourself instead of criticizing.
2. **Be optimistic.** Always believe in yourself. Being an optimist doesn't mean always seeing the brighter side of life. It means viewing your surroundings in a way that allows you to maximize your gifts and strengths and minimize your hesitations and weaknesses.
3. **Forgive and forget.** Your past can control you if you don't control it. If you can, forgive past wrongs and move on. If you have a hard time forgiving or forgetting, consider talking through your emotions with a good friend or counselor, but try not to dwell. Allow freedom and new choices to frame your future.

Answer this: When you view you, what one thing matters most?

PART FOUR

Transformation

Transforming Yourself

"The word 'Action' frees me—the *transformation* is something I cannot explain—too much analysis might destroy it."
— Sophia Loren

The word "transform" is a verb. As with bread, pizza, or apple pie, no matter how you slice it, transformation is about change in character or condition. You can liken it to metamorphosis or conversion, yet personal transformation has a lot to do with whose life you want to be having: yours or someone else's? The bottom line is, it's going to be one or the other.

The concept is fairly simple: We ought to be living life with a single-minded purpose and the intent of getting out of it (and putting into it) as much as we can manage. So how clear are you on what you want out of life? What's hindering your ability to answer this question?

We've all read or heard the following questions: What would you actually do with a million dollars? If you knew you couldn't fail, what would you attempt in life? Or perhaps, what would you do if you knew you were going to be on earth for the next 150 years? Ask yourself, how much time have I dedicated to determining what is actually important to *me*? If you're fortunate to have clear answers, how much time do you focus on the goals in support of what you want? Are the results materializing?

The process of transforming your life so that you are more closely aligned with who you are and what you want can be easily structured. Change *can* be as simple or methodical as you choose. But as Ms. Loren states in the epigraph to this chapter, it *is* important to take action not only now but consistently over time so that you can see, touch, feel, and savor the progress you're making.

As you achieve goals in support of your dream(s), you'll find yourself gaining confidence. You'll realize that the only thing holding you back from living "the dream" was your limiting beliefs. You've undoubtedly heard this phrase countless times. Yet how many more times will you hear it again and defer becoming that amazing butterfly? Consider stepping out of your cocoon, your cozy comfort zone.

What are you actively doing to personally transform yourself?

How Easy Is Change?

"It's almost like an Etch-A-Sketch. You kind of shake it up and we start all over again."

—Eric Fehrnstrom

Such a cool childhood toy, the Etch-A-Sketch—an unsung predecessor to the iPad. Reflecting on the Etch-A-Sketch, I found it an apt metaphor for transformation, for change, for rebirth (in a nonpsychotherapy context).

With an Etch-A-Sketch, you simply created a drawing by turning its two knobs simultaneously. What you created on the screen could be emblematic of anything: your potential, your beliefs, your attitude, or your best stick-figure persona. As you created, you evaluated your results. (Okay, maybe as a child you weren't evaluating, but you get the point.) ☺ And if you didn't like the results, you simply turned the screen upside down, gave it a shake, and started anew.

Looking at our lives, we want

- to feel,
- to learn,
- to grow,
- to stretch,
- to shift,
- to move through,
- to overcome, and
- to embrace and trust our ability to transform ourselves, our family, our community, and perhaps the world.

And you can. Often, it's as easy as reviewing what you have created in your life. If you aren't jazzed with what you're facing, turn it upside down, shake things up a little, and move forward—clean and fresh.

So how can you effect change easily? Here are three starters for your consideration:

1. **Be honest with yourself.** Most people around you won't be honest with you. Human nature steers us away from conflict and hurting others' feelings, so it's important to be able to identify your abilities and limitations and understand how others perceive you. Knowing your strengths and weaknesses can help you adapt.
2. **Focus on what you can do.** People fail because they immediately attach their attention to the negative. They do! (Though some of you may find this surprising.) Change your thinking, and work on the part of your plan that is meaningful to you and others. Do everything you can.
3. **Share yourself.** Too often, we miss the value of sharing our feelings. We don't want to be vulnerable, so we hold back. In doing so, we deprive others of our experience, our learning, and our humanity. When you share your experiences, you increase your empathy, you're more approachable, and you increase your relatability to others.

Finding Your Life's Work

"Our purpose, I believe, is not a thing, place, title, or even a talent. Our purpose is to be. Our purpose is how we live life, not what role we live. Our purpose is found in each moment as we make choices to be who we really are."

—*Carol Adrienne*

This apt quote well expresses one of my life philosophies. Thank you, Carol Adrienne.

As many will attest, sometimes it takes the better part of our lifetimes to discover our life's work, even though we may have been doing it our entire lives without realizing it. Our life's work is not always what we do to earn a livelihood, although we often think it is, and sometimes this way of thinking prevents us from seeing clearly what it is. It may be the work of having children, caring for them, and running a household. The way we know our life's work is by how we feel when we are doing it.

You know these feelings. When you are doing your life's work, you feel an uncanny sense of ease and alignment. This doesn't mean that work is always easy, and it doesn't mean that it's the only work we have to do; it just means that there is a deep conviction within us that tells us we are in tune with our innermost selves. When we are engaged in our life's work, our bodies feel more alive because our energy is feeding us. You may be tired after engaging in your life's work, but rarely are you depleted. You feel a connection with the world, knowing that you belong here and have something important to offer.

Some of you may remember a time when you felt fully engaged in some act of work, service, or creative activity. When you experienced this, it may be that you were simply doing what you were meant to do. On the other hand, if it wasn't an engaging feeling, it may have been time for you to explore what stimulates you—perhaps through volunteering, taking a class, going back to school, or just doing whatever it is you long to try.

Each of you has a calling. When you find it, you owe it to yourself to nurture it, because while it may or may not be your livelihood, it could easily be the key to your well-being.

No flash-in-the-pan here. This is a process. As you continue to explore your life's calling, keep these points in mind:

1. **Be patient.** It takes time. Life is a question that never ends. You may not know right now, and that's okay. Can you let go of needing to know and instead accept the fact that it may take you some time to figure things out?
2. **Ask for guidance.** You don't have to do it all by yourself, especially when you don't know where you're going. Ask for patience and strength. Something greater, stronger, and wiser than you is always here.
3. **Find purpose right here and now.** What's crazy is that we're always looking for passion and purpose somewhere else. It's here; you're living it now—even if you're searching for greater significance in your life and calling. If you haven't yet found those things that speak strongly to you, try focusing on how you can bring presence into your current being.

Appreciating Your Age

"You are as young as your faith, as old as your doubt; as young as your self-confidence, as old as your fear; as young as your hope, as old as your despair."

—Douglas MacArthur

On the *Awakening to Awareness* radio show one week, my guest talked about encore careers and lifelong learning. A university professor who teaches graduate and doctoral students, as well as baby boomers and emerging seniors, he reinforced the idea that aging is relative and often subject to one's own limiting beliefs and feelings. While we are all aging, it doesn't have the same meaning for each of us.

There are valuable insights to absorb and wonderful experiences to savor at each stage of life. Every new decade and every new year brings with it wisdom, transformation, and growth, as well as ends and beginnings. Many people, though, believe there is one age that eclipses the others. They expend energy trying to reach it and, once it has passed, trying to retain it.

But wishing to be younger or older is a denial of the joys that have been and the joys yet to be, as well as the beauty of your life in the present. Holding on to one age can make it difficult to appreciate each new milestone you reach. Taking pleasure in the delights of your age, whether you are in your 20s, 40s, 60s, or 80s, can help you see the magnificence and usefulness of the complex seasons of life.

Think about it: Each new year brings the potential for exciting and unfamiliar experiences. In our 20s, we can embrace the energy of youth and the learning process, knowing it is okay to not have all the answers. As we move through our third decade, we grow more self-assured as the confusion of our young adulthood melts away. We can honor these years by putting aside our fears of aging and concentrating instead on solidifying our values and enjoying our growing emotional maturity.

In our 40s, we become conscious of the wisdom we have attained through life experience and are blessed with the ability to put it to good use. We are not afraid to explore unfamiliar territory or to change. In our 50s, we tend to have successfully navigated our midlife reevaluations and prioritized our lives. In the decades beyond, we discover a greater sense of freedom than we have ever known and can truly enjoy the memory of all we have seen and done.

Aging, however, is about much more than staying physically healthy: It's about maintaining your sense of purpose and your zest for life. Healthy aging means continually reinventing yourself, finding new things you enjoy, learning to adapt to change, staying socially active, and feeling connected to your community.

Here are three tips to keep in mind as *you* age:

1. **Don't fall for the myth that aging automatically means you're not going to feel good anymore.** It is true that aging involves physical changes, but it doesn't have to mean discomfort or disability. While not all illness and pain are avoidable, many of the physical challenges associated with aging can be overcome or significantly mitigated by eating right, exercising, and taking care of oneself.
2. **Many aging adults don't exercise. Yet exercise is vital for healthy aging.** It helps you maintain your strength and agility, gives your mental health a boost, and can even diminish chronic pain. Regular exercise will help you stay physically and mentally healthy and improve your confidence.
3. **As you age, your life will change, and you will lose things that previously occupied your time and gave your life purpose.** But this is not a time to stop moving forward. Later life can be a time of exciting new adventures if you let it. If you're not sure where to get started, try these suggestions: Go on a weekend trip to a place you've never visited, pick up a long-neglected hobby, take a class, join a club, or learn something new (an instrument, a foreign language, etc.).

Try to enjoy the age you are at now, for each age presents its own unique wisdom.

Being Open to Possibilities

"Become a possibilitarian. No matter how dark things seem to be or actually are, raise your sights and see possibilities—for they're always there."

—*Norman Vincent Peale*

Consider Mozart's duet from *The Marriage of Figaro,* a piece that lifted the prisoners' spirits high above prison walls in the film *The Shawshank Redemption:*

> I have no idea, to this day, what those two Italian ladies were singing about. Truth is, I don't want to know. Some things are best left unsaid. I like to think they were singing about something so beautiful it can't be expressed in words and makes your heart ache because of it. I tell you, those voices soared higher and farther than anybody in a gray place dares to dream. It was like some beautiful bird flapped into our drab little cage and made those walls dissolve away. And for the briefest of moments, every last man at Shawshank felt free.

In this way, a vision releases us from the weight and confusion of local problems and concerns and allows us to see more clearly. A vision becomes a framework for possibility.

Possibility, defined, means capable of happening, the capacity for favorable development, or potential.

How many times in life do we find ourselves looking for something to hold on to that gives us safety and a path to travel? The truth is, you can be, do, or have nearly anything you desire. There are infinite possibilities to everything, and the only thing holding you back is yourself. Yes, you are your biggest obstacle. We tend to not move forward with things because we talk ourselves out of them, we fear failure too much, and we are too scared to explore new possibilities.

Heads are nodding, aren't they?

In the middle ages, when lighting a fire from scratch was an arduous process, people frequently carried around a metal box containing smoldering cinder, kept alight throughout the day with bits of kindling. This meant that a man could light a fire with ease wherever he went, because he always carried the spark.

The fact is, our universe is alive with sparks. We have at our fingertips an infinite capacity to light a spark of possibility. Passion, rather than fear, is the igniting force. Abundance, rather than scarcity, is the context. The lesson is this: Give yourself as a possibility to others, and be ready, in turn, to catch their spark. It's about playing together as partners in a field of light.

Being open to possibility is, in part, a transformation—a uniquely significant dance between being and becoming. So when you acknowledge transformation as a movement from being to becoming, into creating, the question, then, is this: How might I think about this or relate to this? Or how might I choose to exist in a way that would yield a different picture and lead me to act in a different way? Possibility is always about the space between what's here and what might be. Given what's happening, what's next? What can I create out of this? What can I learn?

This transformation is a completely different route than one of managing relationships to avoid conflict. Possibility starts with being able to be with things exactly as they are.

Expressing possibility is as easy as consciously using these words:

- may
- might
- can
- could
- maybe
- perhaps
- probably
- how fascinating! (a phrase I love)

In challenging times, people often stop taking risks and making the creative leaps that give life meaning and joy. Yet sometimes, a subtle shift in the conversation, a quiet appeal to our best natures, can make a difference between our stagnating in darkness and living appreciatively in the sunlight.

Possibility presents with a change in attitude. Why not explore and revel in it?!

On a Verge

"We fear our intuitions because we fear the transformational power within our revelations."

—Carolyn Myss

It is documented that dogs have the ability to accurately sense five things: earthquakes, storms, illness, seizures, and labor in pregnant women. Having read this, I wondered whether dogs knew they had these perceiving qualities.

Have you ever sensed that you were on the verge of something big—something radically different or new? How did that sense make you feel? Invigorated? Excited? Hesitant? Perhaps fearful? I pose these questions when I know I am on the verge of significant life changes. I sense this because I trust my intuition—that inner voice that just knows. This isn't precognition, clairvoyance, psychic ability, or impulse. It is simply knowing that even in uncertainty, there is vision associated with a new direction and imminent change.

Some people live for these moments. Others dread them. And there may be an indifferent lot as well. I'm one of the first. When my intuition strongly signals something, I know it is right, and the underlying choices often become strangely easy. It feels healthy. It feels good. It doesn't feel like I'm forcing anything, and there's not a lot of conflict.

Of all the reasons that people should consider using their gut instincts to make big decisions, this may be the best: It frequently leads to choices and outcomes that are fulfilling—decisions that can improve the quality and trajectory of one's life.

If or when you feel you are on the verge of something life changing or perhaps something less significant, here are three considerations that may help:

1. **Honor your intuition.** Honoring your true self takes great courage. It may not be easy, in the short term, to act on what

you sense, but what price do you pay by not listening to it? Trust that nothing is revealed to you intuitively if it is not in your highest interest, even if that means making tough choices in your life. However intuition serves you, it is always in the service of your well-being.
2. **Value time alone.** As you travel the path of intuition and leave behind aspects of yourself and your life that no longer fit, you will need time to be with yourself to help stay grounded in your transition and transformation. Time alone will help you integrate new learning and provide you with guidance along the way. It will also support you to become comfortable without depending on others' approval.
3. **Take in only what is nourishing.** We frequently ignore the inner voice that is continuously providing guidance. We fear what it has to say. Listening to it might strengthen our courage for confrontation or challenge or leave us with a sense of guilt for not doing so. It's your voice! You have the ability to listen objectively and absorb what it's saying compassionately.

PART FIVE

Authenticity

Yes, You, the Authentic One

"The privilege of a lifetime is to be who you really are."
—C. G. Jung

It is joyous to live life authentically, but many in our world do not. It's not for lack of desire; it's just that they aren't sure what living authentically means and how to do it.

There are lots of ways to know thy self. If you're open to giving this more thought *and* some effort, here are seven simple actions you can tap into to strengthen your authenticity:

1. **Meditate.** I know, jump on the bandwagon. Everyone is recommending mediation. But think about it: Before we can listen to the inner core of our authentic selves, we need to learn how to quiet the "noise" that hinders our thoughts by meditating regularly. Did you know you can effectively meditate for five to ten minutes?
2. **Drop the defenses.** If we live so that we can be honest about our lives, we don't need to hide behind a wall of pretense that we often end up believing ourselves. When we bring down the wall, we get to see the world outside and better understand our place in it. The new view can be quite refreshing!
3. **Stop justifying what you do.** You don't need to explain every action. The goal is to know yourself well enough to know that your actions are justified.
4. **Exit "the same old" mentality.** Be willing to do something different. Expose yourself to different ways of thinking; mingle with people who have different ideas and opinions than you. Listen to them, and think about what they say. You don't have to agree with them.

5. **Push your limits safely.** Think of something you've always wanted, but did not dare, to do. Find a way to do it now. Take a hike in the wilderness in silence—maybe a vision quest. Listen to your heart.
6. **Listen to yourself.** How many characters speak through your mouth? Do they truly speak for you and your core values? Or are you parroting someone else's thoughts without the benefit of your own?
7. **Ask for honest feedback.** Then be open to what you hear. We can never know ourselves as others see us if they will not tell us what they observe. Ask two groups of people: those who care for you so much they are willing to risk your anger to help you and those who know you well but who don't care whether you are angry with them.

The American psychologist Abraham Maslow said, "Instead of spending our lives trying to satisfy our deficiency needs, we can become more self-actualizing by creating and pursuing meaningful life purposes. We are self-actualizing if we pursue meanings and values beyond ourselves and our families. We transcend our earlier concern for what other people think and focus instead on being the persons we choose to be. In short, we grow away from conformity toward autonomy."

How are you growing?

Knowing Your True Self

"Be yourself. Above all, let Who you are, What you are, What you believe, shine through every sentence you write, every piece you finish."

—John Jakes

As kids, we live authentically, rarely too afraid or embarrassed to seek out what we want or to speak our minds. As we age, we often put that authenticity aside while we chase our dreams, afraid that it might interfere with achieving success. But we never let that freedom go completely. We may (and I did) conform to society's expectations while secretly nurturing our passions. And we may withhold opinions, though it doesn't change the fact that we had or have them. Yet it's that youthful audacity that, in part, frames who you become. The authentic you is your true self, and in living authentically, you live your truth, projecting who you really are.

Think about it: The easiest way to live your truth is to leave the expectations of others behind and live the way you feel most valuable. Yet why do many find doing this challenging?

Choosing to live an authentic life requires courage and inner strength. And most of us possess these. It takes being selfish, in a healthy way, by doing what you know is best for you, regardless of the opinions of others. It means getting completely honest with yourself and making a heart-strong commitment to be true to yourself. Each of these things is challenging yet doable, right?

If you value personal pursuits, don't feel forced into a certain job just to make enough money to keep up with your neighbors. I did this for decades. And there was little happiness in it. Conversely, if you prize success in what you do and all that comes with it, don't let others' perceptions of what's right for you hold you back. Denying your unique truth can lead to feelings of failure or dissatisfaction because you aren't acknowledging your true self. Sadly, many of us have experienced this.

The following are an action, an exercise, and a factoid associated with being authentic to ponder:

1. **Embrace your negative emotions.** When you numb sadness and pain, you numb happiness and joy. Feeling the depths of your lows enables you to fully feel your highs. To be vulnerable is to be deeply seen. To be vulnerable is to be alive—to exist as your most authentic self.
2. **If you really knew me, you'd know this:** _____.
This is an exercise Tony Robbins gives to seminar participants. Not only does it prompt introspection and allow people to reveal essential aspects of themselves; it also builds trust, credibility, and confidence with the person you are sharing it with. Authenticity does sometimes feel scary, but it builds intimacy.
3. **Authentic people sleep well.** There is something highly diagnostic about peaceful sleep. Someone who sleeps unusually well is someone who is fundamentally in harmony with his or her world. If you consistently fail to sleep well, there can be any number of factors at play that are keeping you out of sync with you most inner, central self. An inability to sleep soundly can signal a deficit in authenticity.

If you are unsure of who the authentic you is, look inward, and ask yourself what your purpose, values, and needs are. Honor your strengths, and don't give in to others' expectations. Finding who you really are and then making the choice to embrace your dreams will take your life in a direction that is meaningful and fulfilling.

You can be your true self, regardless of age. Why not choose to be the authentic you?

Visiting Vulnerability

"The strongest love is the love that can demonstrate its fragility."
—Paulo Coelho

It was early 2003; I was at a quiet Italian restaurant in downtown San Diego having dinner with a friend who I hadn't seen in three months. Being a weeknight, the environment was pleasantly conducive to privacy and conversation. After some time, and at Jeff's prodding, I shared emotional details of my recent past. It was when I was telling him about how they'd stopped my heart from beating for more than two hours during a seven-and-a-half-hour surgery that I lost my composure.

I didn't expect to show that weakness, especially in the presence of someone I viewed as a rock. After all, Jeff was, on the surface, a solid being who epitomized confidence and having one's act together. Maybe it was my being so exposed, maybe it was the red wine, but where the conversation then went was even more unexpected. To make a much longer story shorter, my friend opened up and shared that he was actually a very fragile being.

And there we were: Two accomplished professionals in the corporate world being weak.

What nobody told us was that there is actually a deep inner strength in vulnerability. This may sound contradictory at first, but vulnerability is actually strength in disguise. You know why? Because to be vulnerable, you have to be honest; you have to be the real you. And we were certainly being real.

Being vulnerable isn't just about how you present or project. It's about revealing what you withhold or keep hidden from other people. We all do this to some extent. I'll bet you've never said to a friend, "I just love that I'm insecure." There's the risk that if we reveal our authentic selves, we're likely to be misunderstood, labeled, or rejected. The fear of rejection can be so powerful that some will never let their guards down.

Sometimes it may feel safer to hide our inner feelings in favor of an inauthentic, more confident exterior, but the truth is, people respect vulnerability so much more than a false presence. Playing pretend doesn't ever make you feel good on the inside; it only leaves you feeling like a fraud. And who likes frauds?

Perhaps it's through writing, or maybe it's a function of aging, but ultimately I've realized that I'm still a pretty hard person to get to know. I'm guarded, and I don't break easily, no matter how close I am to people. Maybe you can relate to this. I know that I still keep some people at a comfortable distance, a space that may not render me too exposed.

When you're vulnerable, your heart is wide open. You put your trust in somebody in the form of giving them the most precious thing you have: your heart. When we're vulnerable, we leave ourselves available to be hurt, and people hurt people. So I guess somewhere along the way, I made the decision that vulnerability wasn't for me. I told myself that to be vulnerable would mean to give up my strength, and I didn't want to surrender that. Fortunately, some decisions change with time.

How comfortable are you with putting it all out there—being emotionally butt naked?

It's Okay to Be Alone

"I think it's very healthy to spend time alone. You need to know how to be alone and not defined by another person."

—*Oscar Wilde*

There have been timeless arguments, open-ended debates, and casual conversations about relationships, being connected, and being alone. I am sure compelling cases for each have been and can be made. Yet I believe most would agree that the most important relationship we have in our lives is with ourselves, as challenging as this relationship is.

In June 2014, I wrote a post about the importance of our being connected, from a traditional, social perspective. On the flip side, there is abundant research that suggests blocking off enough alone time is an important component of a well-functioning social life—that if we want to get the most out of the time we spend with people, we need to spend time away from them. When we can shift our expectations with ourselves and others to opportunities for discovery, we open ourselves to new views and unchartered territory.

As we become more chronologically gifted and open to finding what truly makes us feel deeply and strongly, we can then make even more meaningful choices about if and with whom we want to share ourselves and create connections. It is the prospect of losing yourself and finding your way back that makes the experience that much better (yet uncomfortable for some). The outcome of creating space and allowing for time alone is learning more about yourself.

In a recent study, Eric Klineberg, a sociologist at New York University claimed, "There is so much cultural anxiety about isolation that we often fail to appreciate the benefits of solitude." Whether it is for a short period of time or an extended duration, why not consider "the benefits"? Here are three ways to explore and experience time spent alone:

1. **Focus some time on your thoughts (because thoughts do create your reality).** What are your most powerful thoughts? Where are you focusing your attention? Take time alone to become aware of your thoughts. Monitor them, rewrite them, and spend time each day changing negative thought patterns into what you truly believe and want. For those familiar with neuroplasticity, this is how new brain pathways are created.
2. **Schedule solitude.** Proactively allocate time on your calendar to spend time with *yourself*. If you can make time for all the little extras you fit into your day, like stopping at Starbucks, you can schedule time for solitude. It doesn't have to be copious time; just long enough to meditate, focus, relax, produce, and/or think deeply is better than no time.
3. **Check your online communication only once each day.** This means one stop to your inbox, Facebook, and reader. This rule not only allows you to enjoy more quiet time during your work; it forces you to actually meet people when you are feeling social.

The Joy of Being You

"The worst loneliness is to not be comfortable with yourself."
—*Mark Twain*

I had a client who, by any measure, possessed and had achieved everything many people want. Yet he didn't believe he was a good person—someone worthy of all with which he had been blessed. He had unbelievable expectations of himself and self-imposed standards that he (for many years) was unwilling to reconsider. He had pretty much painted himself into a limited corner for growth. He wasn't a good person or a bad person; he just held fast to some cumulative, personal beliefs.

There are choices and actions that lead us in different directions, and it is through those choices and actions that we create our realities. Sometimes we choose or do something that takes us in the opposite direction of the reality we want to create for ourselves. When we do this, we feel bad—uneasy, unhappy, unsure. We might go as far as to label ourselves "bad" when a situation like this arises. Instead of labeling ourselves, though, we could simply acknowledge that we made a choice that led us down a particular path and then let it go, forgiving ourselves and preparing for our next opportunity to choose, and act, in ways that support our best intentions.

Many of us experienced childhoods in which the words "good" and "bad" were used as techniques to control us. We were good if we did what we were told and bad if we didn't. Such discipline undermines a person's ability to find his or her own moral center and to trust and be guided by his or her own inner self. It is important that we grow beyond what we learned and take responsibility for our choices on our own terms.

You are a human being with every right to be here, learning and exploring. To label yourself good, bad, or otherwise is to think too small. What you are is a decision maker, and every moment provides you with the opportunity to move in the direction of your higher self or in the direction of stagnation or degradation.

If you are interested in accepting and being yourself, here are three steps you can take:

1. **Stop before you act.** Whenever or not you are faced with the choice of living your true self in the outside world, stop for a moment. Don't act. Acknowledge your choices. Contemplate their consequences. Ask if the consequence of choosing YOU would be intolerable and how it would feel to deny being yourself. Feel your answers. Then act.
2. **Shift the focus back to you.** The outer world is a reflection of what is going on within us, because we project our own thoughts and feelings onto other people and events. We give it our own meaning. Remember, you can't change other people, the past, or circumstances outside of your control. All you can change is yourself. Shift the focus back onto yourself and realize that you have to power to change your life.
3. **Make little changes.** As you discover little truths about yourself, make little changes. What you might think of as little can have a huge impact on your life. For instance, a slight shift in perspective can color how you choose to approach everything in your life. And that may be all you need to feel significantly happier. I'm not against bold or dramatic change. What's important is understanding why you are making changes.

In the end, only you know the difference. If you find yourself going into self-judgment, try to stop yourself as soon as you can and come back to center. Know that you are not good or bad; you are simply you.

Being Authentic

"Only an authentic life can be a moral life—it can't be any other way."
—*Anonymous*

A while back, I had an opportunity to speak to a group of secondary school administrators. At their request, I addressed the topic of effective public speaking. Following the 90-minute interactive presentation, I invited questions.

One high school principal asked, "When communicating, what is your guiding principle?" Quickly and comfortably I answered, "The truth." I added that being real and genuine when we communicate also has its challenges. For instance, we must face the fears that block our inner truths from emerging, especially the fear of rejection. Also, even when we feel strong enough to communicate the truth, we don't always have clarity about what *is* true for us. Enter authenticity. It just means saying and doing our best to be real. To this audience, I suggested the following: When communicating, think of being authentic as being true to your innermost inspiration, without conformity to the norm, while pursuing a significant life filled with purpose.

So what *is* being authentic? I like this explanation: Being authentic can be defined as unquestionable, congruent living; the moment-to-moment alignment of your sincere thoughts, values, emotions, and actions.

During their formative years, school children are under pressure to conform. For whatever reason, children ridicule or socially reject those who are different. As a result, children begin to mimic others rather than simply and unconsciously being themselves.

Enter ego. Ego wants to get love and approval and knows it can do this by pleasing others. It knows it can achieve this by succeeding in the ways that society expects and accepts.

But stop! Think about how wonderful you feel when you are doing something that you really love, be it singing, creating, or walking aimlessly along the beach. In these moments, what you are doing is in alignment with your true essence. You feel relaxed, forgetting about yourself (and ego), and enjoy just being in the moment. You are your awesome self!

This is how it ought to be—the genuine aspects of our being, whether they are personal gifts or talents. Not only are we here to work, make money, acquire things, and be like everyone else; we are here to experience the fullest expression of our true, authentic selves—who we were destined to be before others shaped (or shape) us into someone else.

What you know about yourself says just as much about the clarity of where you're heading as it does about being authentic. How clear are you on who you really are?

PART SIX

Significance

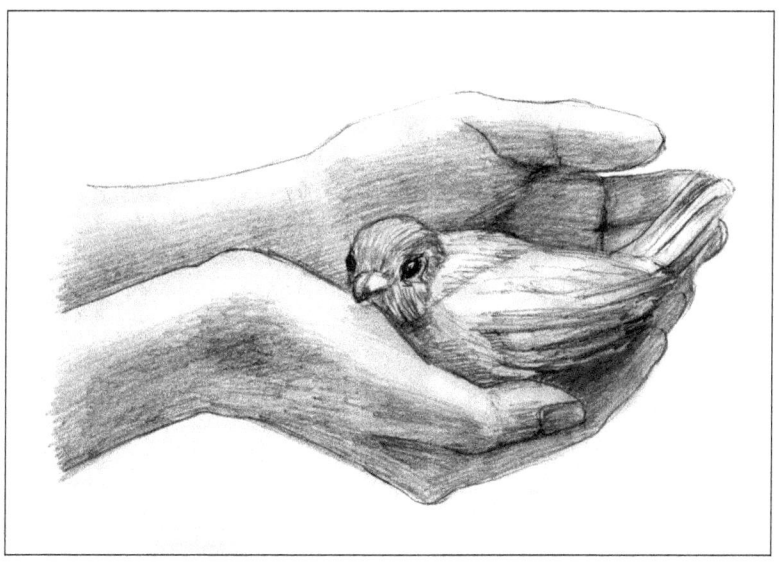

Moments . . . Big and Small

> "I believe that life is a journey, often difficult and sometimes incredibly cruel, but we are well equipped for it if only we tap into our talents and gifts and allow them to blossom."
>
> —Les Brown

I suspect you've had many big moments in your life. Perhaps a significant graduation? The birth of a first child? Paris for your 25th anniversary? But do you remember the small moments, the ones that flash before your eyes? Quite often, those tiny moments are far more significant—like wiping a tear from your grandmother's eye when she buried your grandfather or actually listening to someone distraught about a situation in which you couldn't help or console him or her.

Have you ever known someone whose personal challenges didn't prevent her or him from supporting others? Were you aware that this person's suffering enabled her or him to be even more of an emotional bedrock for others? Maybe it had something to do with her or his having gained perspective on the "important stuff"—things that really matter.

Not everything matters, though we mistakenly think it does. I invite you to reflect on the small, significant moments that have made up your life: not summiting Mount Fuji but breaking bread with a homeless person. Try to remember. Think about what you saw, what you heard, what you felt. What was really happening in those moments? Even more important, what did they do for someone else?

You've likely been invited to answer this question: If you could plan it, how would you spend your last day on Earth? Spending some time with this exercise (by writing down your ideas) will help you focus and yield perspective on what really matters most to you. The question is fairly generic, but your answers will be telling. Dr. Kent Keith, in *The Paradoxical Commandments,* said, "Honesty and frankness make you vulnerable. Be honest and frank anyway." Keith also said, "Give the world the best you have, and you might get kicked in the teeth. Give the world the best you've got anyway."

People search for what is meaningful in their lives, especially when they are broken, confused, frustrated, or simply bored with life. If you're not passively part of a moment, you're creating moments. And many of them are small, seemingly insignificant. But to others, they may be huge!

In a 2011 conversation, a chronologically gifted woman taught me that no matter what I end up doing with my life, I ought to make it significant. Even if your body or your mind is tearing itself apart, consider engaging your senses—your gifts. Start by being present. Look into people's eyes and see them. Ask what matters to them. And celebrate moments with them.

In my work, I invite people to look at their own lives and the day-to-day activities that fill them. Then I ask, "How many of those activities have really mattered in terms of the true reason for your existence?" (And yes, I recognize this depends on one's definition of "true reason.")

I have one simple suggestion today, an old-fashioned one. Consider demonstrating the importance of a relationship by calling someone just to see how they're doing. To be honest, I receive very few calls from people who don't have a self-serving agenda. Those who do call because they genuinely care about me stand out. Think about it: How often do people call (not text or e-mail) you just to say hi or to find out what's going on in your life? Your call may end up being a significant moment for them.

Things along Your Path

"Each man's life represents a road toward himself."
—Herman Hesse

Last month I drove up to the Jemez Mountains to hike. There was plenty of winding road to travel before I arrived at my chosen trail head. It was a beautiful Indian summer day, and my awareness was unusually heightened. As I traveled, I noticed a lot of "stuff" in and along the road—makeshift memorials, potholes, unusual boulders, worn tires, and abandoned personal belongings—some of which was uncomfortably close to the driving lane. When hiking, I thought about what I had previously seen and wondered if there was a message in all of it.

It seems the road was a metaphor for the paths that each of us is on—that there is often a lot in or along our path. Some of the "stuff" is obvious, and some of it is less visible yet still there. We don't always see the smaller things in life, even though they can be as significant as larger, avoidable objects. Items along our path can represent knowledge, wisdom, guidance, or reminders. If we are aware of these objects, we can avoid them, or we can tune in to their relevance.

Missing, ignoring, or misunderstanding signs doesn't mean they disappear; they just keep showing up until we see them. When it comes to our personal path, two things are essential: what is seen and what is not seen but needs to be. Finding meanings is unnecessary; learning lessons, draining; and knowing what decisions to make, frustrating. We need only trust our intuitions, our knowledge, and our hearts to safely guide us.

When I returned home that night, I thought again about the significance of the things in and along the road and wondered about the message. What I realized was that we are often served reminders to be aware and to stay focused on our path.

What is in your road today? Is it what needs your awareness, requires your focus, or reminds you of your gifts and purpose?

Here are three thoughts to consider as you travel *your* path:

1. **Every question is answered.** Even thoughts that aren't formed into questions but are brewing in your mind are answered. Be open to how the answers come and the direction in which they point.
2. **Negative emotions, frustration, and weak anticipation are symptoms of debris on the road.** Open your eyes, see it, and stay true to the clarity of your vision and purpose.
3. **On the road, struggling and being indecisive are just ways to damage yourself.** Look for the clear and open path and trust it.

In Those Five Minutes

> "Treat people as if they were what they ought to be and you can help them to become what they are capable of becoming."
>
> —J. W. von Goethe

The firefighter at your door sternly states you have five minutes to gather whatever you choose and evacuate your residence. A physician summons you with the news that you probably have no more than five minutes to be with a dying loved one. You're entering emergency surgery and are asked to consider an organ-donor consent form. You're on a flight when the captain instructs passengers to brace for impact.

In times of uncertainty, danger, or impending loss, we are forced to transcend the thinking that usually dominates our everyday awareness. Without notice, you might have to make lightning-quick decisions to which you haven't given much prior thought. Shifting from the trivial to the critical usually exceeds your brain's speed limit. And you're likely unfocused and unsure about what to do. In those precious moments, are the following important?

- your degree(s)
- your age
- technological conveniences
- what you control
- social media
- what's on the news
- your investments
- what you look like
- global politics
- how you're acting
- material possessions

I suspect not. You're dealing with a racing mind, feeling physically exhausted and depleted, and scrambling to make sense of the seemingly unfathomable. What can you say, think, do? Is this a space in which you anticipated being?

When standing at such an edge, uncertain about the future, one can hope to draw strength from knowing what really matters—for those five minutes . . . what to grab, what to say, how to react, and how to decide, with compassion.

There's a purpose here. It's to encourage thought about what you value and to invite you to align your life with same. Because possessing clarity about what matters, matters!

In anticipation of having only five minutes, would confirmation of any of the following help?

1. **Be yourself.** When living as a passionate, inspired being, the only challenge greater than learning to walk a mile in someone else's shoes is to walk a lifetime comfortably in your own. Let your heart lead and take your brain along. When you're clear and comfortable about what matters to you, making tough decisions can come more easily.
2. **Be a front-runner.** Associate with others who share your values and aspirations. Don't find yourself in a position where social gravity draws you into an unenlightened world and obscures who you are, what you know to be important, and how you choose to confidently embrace being at choice.
3. **Don't stop remembering why.** Many of us have tendencies to lose touch with what we loved as a child. The social pressures of adolescence and later professional pressures squeeze the passion out of people. Remember what you enjoy doing, with whom you enjoyed doing it, and why. You only need to be good at being and valuing you and being there for others.

Humility Helps

"I long to accomplish a great and noble task, but it's my chief duty to accomplish humble tasks as though they were great and noble."
—Helen Keller

I used to think I was important. And I struggled with believing that I was worthy. For each of us, the notion of humility as a virtue brings numerous images to mind. We tend to envision those rare individuals who humbly bear life's struggles while downplaying their own strengths. Yet humility is also associated with people whose insecurities compel them to judge themselves unfavorably. The true definition of humility, however, does not precisely correspond with either of these images.

Humility is not passivity. Rather, it is an utter lack of self-importance. Individuals who embody the concept of humility appreciate that each human being occupies a unique place within the sphere of development. Though they can take pride in their own accomplishments, they also understand that the people they interact with each day are as valuable and have as much to offer the world as they themselves do.

As you consider your humility, keep in mind that to be humble is to accept that while there will always be people more and less advanced than you, each individual can provide you with insights that further your personal growth. Recognizing this is a matter of opening yourself up to the fact that not only do others think differently than you, but their life experiences have shaped them in very different ways than yours have shaped you.

This means that while you may have a greater understanding in some areas, others will always be able to teach you something. When you cultivate a genuine yearning to know what skills and talents those you encounter have been blessed with, you cannot help but learn humility. You instinctively understand that emotions like envy breed resistance that prevents you from growing and that being flexible in your interactions with others will help you connect with unexpected mentors.

Think about times when you talk to your older relatives. It can be time-consuming, repetitive, and at times underwhelming. But it is important to acknowledge that they often spent their lives contributing to raising you (whether directly or indirectly). When you practice humility, you want to become as accomplished and evolved as you can possibly be, yet you are willing to submit to the expertise of others to do so. You understand the scope of your attitudes, yet you choose to dismiss arrogance from your attitude, and you can distinguish the value you possess as an individual while still acting in the interests of others.

Humility, simply put, is a form of balance in which you can celebrate your own worth while believing that every other person is just as worthy as you.

If you're looking for ways to be more humble in your life, consider these tips:

1. **As a human being you need to be aware of your faults and misgivings.** You need to know that you are not unsurpassed. It's okay to not be perfect and accept your weaknesses.
A better self-awareness will help you be more humble in life.
2. **Learn to say, "I don't know."** It's hard, for whatever reason, to answer someone with "I don't know." Probably because all of the world's information is at our fingertips, not knowing something seems like an unacceptable excuse or not a legitimate answer. Life's full of questions to which we simply don't have answers. Say, "I don't know," listen, then learn.
3. **Serve someone.** We instinctively resist serving because we sometimes believe there is a direct relationship between serving others and our being self-important—an "it's more about me and less about them" mind-set. Bring someone a cup of coffee, run an errand for a friend, or give away some money.

Most of us still have some learning and practicing to do. Do you agree?

A Meaningful Life Trumps

"Life is not infinite, but its potential is. Embrace every second and you'll triumph over compunction."

—Eric Tonningsen

It took years, but I finally figured it out. When you're not happy, unfulfilled, or not living a meaningful life, you ought to (I really wanted to type *must*) make a change. If you remain a slave to cultural expectations and the trappings of money, power, status, and/or perceived success, you've left a void in your life. I told myself, "If you're truly unhappy with your job, move on. Find a way to pursue your passion and mission in life." So I left a world in which I prostituted myself to shareholders, made good money, traveled the world, and had whatever I wanted. What was missing was meaning and significance. And I knew this for some time.

I'm not telling you to quit your job; you may love your job. But are you happy? Essentially, we are happy when we get what we want. But when our happiness outweighs meaning in our lives, something's disproportionate. I believe happiness without meaning characterizes a relatively shallow, self-absorbed life in which things go well, needs and desires are easily satisfied, and difficult affairs are avoided.

When I decided to step out of my professional comfort zone and into the unknown, it was terrifying and exhilarating, surreal, and at times indescribable. Suddenly, I was accountable to myself. For the first time in my life, I wasn't that highly confident being. Yet I knew I was heading in the right direction.

Days after I left the traditional workforce, I came across this Joseph Campbell quote, which has guided and inspired me ever since: "The privilege of a lifetime is being who you are." I have personally added to this quote, "and what you can still be."

If you are contemplating a major life shift, how might you contribute in more meaningful ways, and how would living a life of greater significance change you? The following are three anchoring thoughts as you explore meaning:

1. **Figure out what defines you.** You've dreamed for most of your life. You have a vision of "what could be." It can still be achieved. Personally, I have a lot of life left and plans to effect meaningful change. Sure, everything won't work out just as I had planned. But I can focus on being ready for whatever opportunities (and challenges) come my way. Dreams and visions can define us, even if they don't turn out exactly as we hoped.
2. **Question whose approval you are seeking.** Like it or not, we're all sometimes guilty of relying on others' opinions to feed our feelings and self-worth. While approval and compliments from others can feel great, seeking them all the time can be unhealthy. They can turn into self-fulfilling cycles of negative feelings. When you start on a self-discovery journey and pursue what you want to do, you take ownership of your life and begin to realize that it matters what *you* think about you.
3. **Remember that you have a right to pursue your passions.** Don't ever let anyone convince you that pursuing your passion is impractical. Passion is what brings meaning and value to your life. The pursuit of your passion(s) directly affects the quality of your life experience. Don't allow your passions to drift into the "maybe someday" file. Life is too short to settle for anything less than passion.

What Really Matters

"Do not care overly much for wealth or power or fame, or one day you will meet someone who cares for none of these things and you will realize how poor you have become."

—*Rudyard Kipling*

A friend shared the following with me. It was written in 2003 by American speaker and lecturer Michael Josephson:

Ready or not, someday it will all come to an end.

There will be no more sunrises, no minutes, hours or days.

All the things you collected, whether treasures or baubles, will pass to someone else.

Your wealth, fame and temporal power will shrivel to irrelevance. It will not matter what you owned or what you were owed.

Your grudges, resentments, frustrations and jealousies will finally disappear. So, too, your hopes, ambitions, plans and to-do lists will expire.

The wins and losses that once seemed so important will fade away. It won't matter where you came from or on what side of the tracks you lived, at the end.

It won't matter if you were beautiful or brilliant. Even your gender and skin color will be irrelevant.

So what will matter? How will the value of your days be measured? What will matter is not what you bought but what you built, not what you got but what you gave.

What will matter is not your success but your significance. What will matter is not what you learned but what you taught.

What will matter is every act of integrity, compassion, or sacrifice that enriched, empowered or encouraged others to emulate your example.

What will matter is not your competence but your character.

What will matter is not how many people you knew, but how many people will feel a lasting loss when you're gone.

What will matter is not your memories but the memories in those who loved you. What will matter is how long you will be remembered, by whom and for what.

Living a life that matters doesn't happen by accident. It's not a matter of circumstance but of choice.

It is my belief that we can be who we are and fulfill our incredibly unique purposes if we so choose.

How can you really matter to others? There are countless ways. Here are three worth pondering:

1. **Tell the people in your life how you feel about them.** If this doesn't come naturally to you, all the more reason to do it more often. It will become natural. "You matter" is what many want to hear. These work well, too: "I'm happy to see you," "You mean so much to me," "Your contribution to the team is immeasurable," and "I so appreciate you." The language of mattering is universal. Tell people, and tell them often, how much they matter.
2. **Remember that sometimes following your calling means leaving the ones you love behind.** This is a tough one. Sometimes it's not our role in this life to be the best sibling, spouse, or friend, because we're here to contribute in different and unique ways. Honor what's true for you rather than falling in line with what society implies ought to really matter.
3. **Talk about others.** Few like those in the family, at work, or at the party who only talk about themselves, their interests, their accomplishments, and their importance, right? You become far more interesting and important when you talk about the exciting things other people are doing, trying, creating, writing, and sharing. Doing so gives you the opportunity to establish yourself as someone who is learning from others and growing because of it.

PART SEVEN

How

Getting from Here to There

"We are our choices."

—Jean-Paul Sartre

Making the visible invisible is entertaining. That's what a magician does when making an object "disappear." However, making the invisible visible is a far more impressive feat, and you have done that every time you have taken a dream, waved your magic wand of ambition at it, and created something in the physical world for all to view.

You already have accomplished so much. But you know there is still more ambition inside of you—so much more you want to do, so much more you can do, so much more you will do. How? Walk along with me...

For thousands of years, generations have been surrounded by amazing knowledge and possibilities for personal growth. Whether it is time, focus, or not understanding, the applications and uses of knowledge and learning are the hardest part of change. We read, listen, and learn, but it doesn't seem to make it into our reality. All the knowledge and possibilities in the world are useless if we don't cross the bridge from knowing to living.

The bridge is a path over or through the gap between where we are and where we want to be. To cross the bridge and expand the possibilities of living better begins with awareness of what brings us satisfaction now and what would bring us more. Clarifying what is creating the gap between where we are and where we want to go begins the crossing of that bridge. Honest awareness makes this possible.

With expanded awareness, we can spend time and energy exploring and discovering the concepts, ideas, and strategies that help us to close the gap and cross the bridge. We have to reflect, consider, and imagine how new ideas or actions could change us. This is a new knowledge, and if we can't see the knowledge expressed in our reality, we'll be stuck on the bridge. And we all know how frustrating that can be.

With clarity and knowledge, followed by exploring our possibilities, we can make choices. We only have to choose an action, a pattern, or an opportunity to effect change. Keep repeating the new choice, and the easier that change will become. It won't be long before the new knowledge becomes the old knowledge and more possibilities for growth are recognized—and a new gap will appear.

It's a cycle, a constructive loop. Every day becomes a new adventure in expanding, enjoying, and discovering as the bridges get crossed. With each bridge crossing from knowledge to reality, we learn to enjoy the process as our understanding and potential expand.

Now ask yourself, are you contemplating crossing, are you presently traversing, or have you successfully bridged a recent gap? Is it somehow enabling you to realign your life?

ACKNOWLEDGMENTS

I want to recognize a small community that has inspired the writing of and helped to frame *Awakening to Awareness*. Each individual has traveled and endured a special journey. Having, at one time or another, made conscious choices about how to live unselfishly, these people (some unknowingly) prompted a realignment of my life with what really matters.

Jeff Hawkinson embodies and exemplifies kindness. In the more than 13 years we've known each other, Jeff continuously amazes and warms me with his gracious and caring ways. I frequently thought of Jeff when crafting blog posts, some of which can be found in this book. With kindness being a facet of what really matters, what Jeff personifies is a trait to which many can aspire.

Jane Miner, Ed.D., was my first life coach. Jane was instrumental in helping me identify and embrace my talents, or as she calls them, "personal gifts." Jane both encouraged and inspired me to pursue my passions, regardless of what others might think or say. Jane was also instrumental in highlighting and trusting my intuitive abilities—which continue to serve me well.

Eleanor Tonningsen, my mother, is at her core, the epitome of compassion. It has taken me many years (far too long) to see and learn the importance of (proportionately) placing others' needs and comforts ahead of my own. My mother has been doing this for as long as I can remember, and it pleases me to profess my forward-going commitment to emulate her actions.

Bailey and Logan (yes, my black labs) are fountains of unconditional love. On the best and on the worst of days, they bring laughter into my life without my ever asking. They simply care for and please me, no questions asked. They are free of expectation and soothe me in their own unique ways. If only we humans could regularly mirror our animal companions' giving ways.

On the self-belief front, I must credit my indefatigable Spirit. If it weren't for my Spirit and its mission of "getting things right" while coupled with my body in this earthly life, I'd be measurably rudderless. It's my Spirit that repeatedly whispers that I can do anything I want to do . . . be anything I want to be. And I will do what truly matters!

And Craig Duswalt, the guy who encouraged me (and countless others) to host my own radio show, to launch a blog, to write a book, and to speak in public—to share my authentic stories. With this book, I have now accomplished all four of his recommendations. And as a professional speaker, there are many more meaningful messages to come.

www.ingramcontent.com/pod-product-compliance
Lightning Source LLC
Chambersburg PA
CBHW071749080526
44588CB00013B/2194